People of The Future/Day

Youssef Khalim

Copyright © 2012 Youssef Khalim

All rights reserved.

ISBN: 978-0-9787810-2-6
ISBN-13: 978-0978781026

DEDICATION

To: Larisa Khalim (The real or ideal soul-mate: inspiration).

Tonya Tracy Khalim and

Runako Soyini Khalim, (my most beloved daughters).

Mother and Grandmother and Great-grandmother, (my most beloved maternal biological ancestors, and spiritual antecedents).

M. A. Garvey (one of my 7 M's: my role models).

Youssef Khalim II; III (my most beloved sons).

Father and Grandfather and Great-grandfather, (my most beloved paternal biological ancestors, and spiritual antecedents).

To: The Forerunners and Reincarnation sources (beloved biological ancestors and spiritual antecedents), and

The Almighty (our Spiritual Father), from whence we come.

CONTENTS

	Acknowledgments	i
1	Of Women	1
2	Marsha (Ahsram)	Pg 2
3	Spring Wind Now	Pg 3
4	Sandra	Pg 4
5	A Sister	Pg 5
6	Of Marriage –Vow	Pg 6
7	Of Destiny & Struggle	Pg 7
8	Of Liberation	Pg 8
9	Som'n 'Bout Land	Pg 9
10	Uhuru (Meaning Freedom)	Pg 10
11	Traitors	Pg 12
12	People of the Future/Day	Pg 13
13	Media	Pg 14
14	TV in America	Pg 15
15	Road to Freedom	Pg 16
16	Haiti	Pg 17
17	Lovers Fight?	Pg 18
18	My Blood	Pg 19
19	Vigil	Pg 20
20	Of Food	Pg 21
21	Of Ancestors & Offspring	Pg 22
22	Incarnation	Pg 23

23	Runako	Pg 24
24	Of Love Affairs	Pg 25
25	James L. Robinson II	Pg 26
26	Of Light & Frivolity,	
	Songs to Sing or Read	Pg 27
27	Light	Pg 28
28	Our Music	Pg 29
29	Style	Pg 30
30	If	Pg 31
31	Love Now	Pg 32
32	I Love You	Pg 33
33	About the Author,	
	And Other Books	Pg 34

ACKNOWLEDGMENTS

To: The Forerunners and Reincarnation sources (beloved biological ancestors and spiritual antecedents), and

The Almighty (our Spiritual Father), from whence we come.

1 Of WOMEN

Women are of the
Substance which keeps the
Worlds a-spinning.

2 MARSHA (AHSRAM)

There are no songs,
No thoughts, no tantalizing miazma*colors,
There are no picture words to picture you.

No lights reflect,
No cameras can pan, intake.
No pensive moods can feel your feel.
No myriad Kaladi* paints of brush,
No strings of lyre,
No sounding trumpets harping grandly:
There are no picture words to picture you.

No sunsets catch,
Nor sunrise match
Your splendid splendor.

No sweet and scented
Bright transcendent
Flowery flower's on a par with you.

No eloquence,
No heralds would announce,
No silvery words to speech,

No monuments,
No golden jewels,
No priceless prize:
There are no picture words to picture you.

Were it be known,
You must be felt: be known, be had.

There are no picture words to
Picture you.

*Miazma- Liquid appearing prismatic conditions created by bright light and unparallel transparent planes or water vapor.

*Kaladi-Multifaceted.

3 SPRING WIND NOW

She let me be
She let me free

And now so high
I, butterfly

Can taste
The other flowers.

4 SANDRA

You be like dancing, sliver colors
Gliding easy,

And crisp-bright clever acts
And feats of poise.

You be like dainty svelte
Virgin gardens

And stately emblem flowers
Budding fresh.

You be like masterpiece
Envisioned

And dreams by saintly genius
Souls.

You be like sounds of velvet
Thronged in Sunbeams

And life aglow caress(ed)
EV-E-R Y
Note:

You be like Ophir's prizes
And sought like Gilead.

5 A SISTER

Said she danced
And I'd be interested
T' see.

But I'm not looking forward
To it,

Cause when she walks
It's musical
Ballet

Sculptured majesty,
Smooth, flowing,
Regal,
Natural dance.

6 OF MARRIAGE - VOW

I pledge to love you
Stand beside you
At all times,
Especially when you
Need me.

& I pledge patience,
Loyalty, respect, Charity/affection.

I pledge my soul

& mind & body
Beg to serve
And warm assist you
To enjoy of life & living.

Likewise, I pledge
To the creation
Of our love,
Forever.

7 OF DESTINY & STRUGGLE

8 OF LIBERATION

"What must the people say of the fruits
Of their labor?"

Say: "After all work is done toward the
End result, forces of the Universe
Complete what is needed; I am the
Manifest force of the Universe; my
Work is not in vain."

9 SOM'N 'BOUT LAND

Hey, brotherman,
Dig this rap
'bout land:

If you can
Show me man
Something
Not from land.

There's thread
 From land
& lead
From land,
&
Light & gas &
Wood from land.

Leather goods
& shoes from
Land.
&
Silver, gold,
Diamonds
From land.

Glass from land,
& brass from land
A mule from land,
Jack.

Tell me man,
Don't we need
Some land?

Say, have you seen some food from air?
No, food from land.

Have you seen
A man from
Air?

No, man from land.

Have you seen plane land on air?
No, land on land.

Can you build
Concrete without
Some land?

Now,
Canaan land
Was stolen
Land,
The Promised Land.
& Ameri-can on stolen land.

Tell me man,
We rap 'bout
Land,

Now,
Ain't it time
To take -
Our land?

10 UHURU (MEANING FREEDOM)

Across the Horn of Aden
Comes this query:
Uhuru? Uhuru?
Uhuru yet?
Are you ready for Uhuru
Yet?

Over the snake-tongued
Nile this query:

Tis like monotone's
Entreaty,

Querying, question'ng
The oft asked query

Of the Sons across
Time's spanning:

Are you ready
Ready yet?

Atop Mt. Kenya, stride Ruwenzoris,
Amid the thunder
Of the falls

Across savanna, steppe
Grass land,
Half way cross Sahara's
Sunness,

Seeps crescendo
Now tis louder,
Comes the query
Ever questioning:

Are you ready,
Ready yet?

Where Niger flow
Stops, Kongo starts
& ocean frames
Her ample vastness,
Comes the query
In shriek & scream,

As if it bad some
Nostrils blared,

And bones stitched
O'er with blood
& tissue, lymph, & marrow
Heart & gut,

And out its bowels
It now must shout:

Thundering's pinnacle
Lighting's clap,

And earthquake's
Roar:

This selfsame
Query: Uhuru,
Uhuru, Uhuru
Yet?

Are Sons
Ready for Uhuru yet?

Stirred, provoked
Incensed at last
About this freedom
(Uhuru) yet?

The Sons now answer
Uhuru's quest,
Response to query
Uhuru yet.

Say:
Time's Uhuru!
Freedom's now

So know the time!

Now pass the word:
Uhuru, fight,
& fight, fight
Fight!

Cause time,
Uhuru.

Freedom's now!
The God commands Sons fight!

Say:
Cling with self
You shall prevail.

Uburu's here
To cleanse the
Stench engulfs
All heavens,
Fouls the depths
Of hell.

Repair the

Kind to kind.

& build a
Love of self,

Re-tear &
Rip apart,
Unsheathe

The gleaming splendor
Soul defiled.
The time's Uhuru
Freedom's now,
So know the time.

Now,
Blood must run
Thick, red & steamy
Throughout the sidewalks
Of the world

Unless the world
Be turned around.
& never, never
Never, ever
Shall
Sons be bound
Again (by thugs & bandits)
Kidnapers, rapers:
Scum that stole the earth.

So, fight hold
Steady,

The time's Uhuru
Freedom's now!

So know the time!

Tensile your
Spine &
Blow your horn,
But wield your thunder
Bolt!
Shine Son!
Uhuru's era's
Here
Again
And peace will
Rain mid pyramids,
In Ethiop-land
'Cross the measure
Of the vastness

No force can stay
Uhuru reign!

11 TRAITORS

Sometimes it
Pains
To hear
The Un-US
People,
Ones who
Stab US in the back,
Betray US,
Join our enemy,

Then based on
Fact that they have
COLOR,

Like US,
How the hell can
They prescribe a
Cure, or criticize
US?

Better that they stay
Far
Clear
& leave US to our own,
& this for them too!

12 PEOPLE OF THE FUTURE/DAY

We be the Afrikan American
People

Future people of
The day

Becoming people of
The Sun,

Retiring people of
The cold.

The high vibration
Emotion, feel

Of wavelength
Purple/blue
Is gold.

Displacing red, computer, detail
Materialist, money, cold.

We be

Group people
Group!

Group people
Group.

The future
Day
Is
Now!

13 MEDIA

Time, times herald,
You lie, you cheat,
You falsify my story.

CBS or NBC,
You show distortion.

Backwards, forward,
Anyway you dare,
You show the lie.

No,
Truth is not your object,
Objectivity not your goal.

You people have to learn
To learn: the world's a boomerang

& what you sow
Will build you up or kill.

14 TV IN AMERICA

Consumption of time,
 pollution of mind

 Innuendo
 Propaganda

 Tools of tools
 Of power (must)
 Change.

15 ROAD TO FREEDOM

(We are the first free generations).
Though you chained my mother's mom
In chains, she wept
& vowed a vengeance through me.

Said the gods must
Have a plan,
A lesson to be learned
& steeled her will
& passed it on to me.

She said her forbears, victim.
Hostages of war, Disciples/struggle!

(The gods must have a plan & lesson to be learned).

Wait.

Then, & now we
Understand the lesson,
Plan!

We learned
& we can say
Never again,

 Nev-er.

We will be free!

16 HAITI

Land of Dessalines,
Dashed ashore 'mongst alabaster,
Rest the sable soaring seed.

The sky of Haiti,
Tucked amidst the bone dried grave,
Revive the moist green Aden.

The mountains capped,
Chiseled like jutting tender breasts,
Guard gold island cross the sun.

The victory soil,
Hovered over by ancestor gods,
Be tread sole bare, or planted.

Brave peasant gentry,
Blest with liberty and freedom,
Viv 'La Haitian Afrikans.

17 LOVERS FIGHT?

There's just no
Time...
To fight w/you & enemy too.

I will not fight you anyway,
The one I love your
Role:

To give & take of love & share of life;
To complement
The(e)
Struggle,
See?

If you so filled
With fight, & have this excess time,

Go,
End
Our
Enemy!

18 MY BLOOD

You be
Unnatural
With your dyed & fried
& colored
Head
 & Hair
 &
SELF,
Blood.

19 VIGIL

Lest you pollute
Yr/self
& make us suffer,
Beware
Unnatural
Unclean
People
Habits/things/ideas,
Lest you pollute
Yr/self
& make us suffer.

20 OF FOOD

Consuming habits
Take a lot of fruits
& vegetables,

At times & spells
Some feasts in meats,
Not swine.

There's fish or cheese,
Likewise dry wines,
At times.

Candy, nuts, ice cream
In spells.

&
Air is good.

21 OF ANCESTORS & OFFSPRING

22 INCARNATION

Each generation owes the previous generation for
What it has.

Or the previous generation owes the current
For what it loses. In this manner material
Things are passed.

Therefore, we are the incarnate representative,
Heir, executor, creditor, & debtor of previous
& future generations.

Spiritual forces execute harmony, balance &
Justice-and always operate.

Material is but the manifesting spirit-
For expression & development.

Work & attention should concentrate on current
Circumstances & recognize past & future consequences
Of ancestors & offspring.

23 RUNAKO

She showed me
Lots about
Myself.

She sketched
Or showed
Her drawings.

Sought
Applause!

She was so
Doggone sweet,
Said yes sir, yes ma'am, thank you,
May I help?:
In voice so soft & pleasing.

Now, then again
She was so
Vicious:

Lil' fragile thing
Would kick & bruise her sister
Signify &
Aggravate,
Taunt & mock
Verbal attack,
Chattering ceaseless.

When I confronted
Child like father:
"What the....
Stop!
I'll break your neck,"

The fearless brat
Would glare
Behind
Time-out
Offense,

Then go
& seek her
Own world
By herself,
Serene,
Without me.

In-
de-
pendent
Rebel.

She wouldn't
Budge
Iota,
Do,
Until
She

Pleased:
God
Gave
Runako.

24 OF LOVE AFFAIRS

We wed,
No ceremony
(Several times).

We fought
& hassled.

Communicated
Lots,
Read to
Each other.

We walked
Together, holding hands.

We kissed
Quite often,

& understood
All possible knowing
'Bout each other
For a father-daughter.

25 JAMES L. ROBINSON II

The sun rose in your smile
& you were dearest to my
Breast & heart.

Your cry or laugh
Was mine because
How could us one,
Be part?

You lived much too hurriedly
Developed much too fast.

Was it because you knew too well
That life on earth wouldn't last?

I know you went to a better
Home in a better part of heaven.

Thus justice reins & our score is
Made somewhat more even.

Now when we meet again, if you
Know me before I you, Say, "How are you
This time?" Say, "How've you been through time?"
And then say, "I love you."

OF LIGHT & FRIVOLITY, SONGS TO SING OR READ

27 LIGHT

Did you ever
Think of light,

Of fireside light
Of sun-star light,

Of flickering, flashing
Dashing swirling curling
Dancing lite?

Did you see the
fireworks light?:

The shimmering, glimmering
Blaring, glaring zillions
Showers
Light.

& have you known
The astral light?

The nectar, peachy, homing, roaming,
Glowing, ebbing
Waxing fading
Lite?

The strident light
Of red or blue
Sirening screaming
Light, invokes a fright
Like death of night.

But happy light
& fun-filled light
Create a blithesome
Lite.

There's disco light,
& groovy turning, spinning
Funning lite.

A puckering against each other &
Separating, churning blue to
Green to orange, tilting angles, lilting
Angles;

 Light,
Teasing the eye.

28 OUR MUSIC

Our Music
Swells the heart
Like (Steve is Wonder) ful
A Trane gives
Miles of Koolish
Pleasure,

Hot Chocolate,
N' Cole Send Me,
A 're tha's soul when swinging;

Dells Nancy W/song
Count the Basie:
Earth, Wind & Fire Emotions
N' Manhattan(s); Jackson, 5 LTD:
(I'd use up all my pen before the End.)

A Howling Wolf,
Say: "Listen!"

It's sure to swell your heart.

29 STYLE

I write
So subtle
Get real tender,
Sweet.

I get so
Soft & lithe,
I whisper....

Start
Or stop Turn/whirl or Glide,
I
Hit
Real hard or slam & growl or roar,

I twist,
Attack so sudden,
Inch away & counter,
Smile,
Play opossum, feint.

Organic life flows through me.

I pin the deep emotions,
Sense & paint the slightest throb.

I lift you to the highest heights
To taste of ecstasy
Or trudge along the
Pitts of bell to feel the
Weight of pain.

I wrap it up
Summation wit a
Tease of writ.

30 IF

If you love me,
Do it.

If you care,
Produce.

If you feel,
Then touch me.

If you want
Me, take.

If you're sweet,
Then sweeten.

If you're fire,
Burn.

Don't take all
The seasons.

Show me &
I'll learn.

31 LOVE NOW

I want to love
Before the love
I feel for you
Goes fleeing.

Something we say
Or do today
May kill my love.

And then there's
Time & circumstance.
The dream I (am)
May fade (away).

While love is strong
We can't go wrong

And we can capture
The greatest rapture
While we still care.

So let's not wait.
The gate to heaven
Stands before us.

And we should love
While love is strong
& we still care.

32 I LOVE YOU

Sometimes I love you much too much
That kind of love can get you hurt.

I care so much and want you so
These things I tell, you shouldn't know.

Your love may be just like the rest:
Take all my love & move your nest.

33 ABOUT THE AUTHOR, AND OTHER BOOKS

Youssef Khalim obtained Unity in yoga on about 7/20/80. He says, "We will recombine into one faith, Judaism, Christianity, and Islam." He has been able to "see" and experience some amazing information about USA presidents Jefferson, Lincoln, and Obama; and also Prophets Moses, Muhammad, and Solomon - in visions, lucid dreams, and in meditation. Khalim makes reincarnation (resurrection) central again in our western religions. He resides in the Chicagoland area. And he is the father of Tonya, Runako, and Noah. See his books on the following websites: http://lulu.com and http://sunracommunications.com

Other Books

Youssef Khalim's books include *You Are Too Beautiful; I Love You Back; You Look So Good; The Resurrection Of Noah; Jubilee Worldwide; Lara, Forever; Tanisha Love; Galina, All About Love; I Call My Sugar, Candie; Natalia, With Love; Svetlana, Angel Of Love; Lori, My Dream Girl*; *Love of My Life*; and *The Second Coming!*